Praise for:

The True Power of Girls

"Grace DeLynne is wise beyond her years. It is refreshing to see this young lady's leadership and hunger to inspire the world. *The True Power of Girls* is a book that will help girls of all ages find their true selves and live confidently for their dreams!"

— Les Brown, World-Renowned Motivational Speaker, Best-Selling Author of *You've Got to Be Hungry*

"*The True Power of Girls* makes you want to go out into the world and live your dreams without any fear. This book is a beautiful guide for girls everywhere to realize their full potential and all of the magic that resides within them! Grace DeLynne is a clever communicator and a shining representation of the true power of girls!"

— Renée Marino, Best-Selling Author of *Becoming a Master Communicator*, Communication Coach, Speaker, and Mary Delgado in Clint Eastwood's *Jersey Boys* film

"Grace is a standout in her generation! Her didactic nature and her pervasive vision for social influence are evidenced on every page of this book. *The True Power of Girls* is a strategic guide to helping girls find peace, develop purpose, and discover the many ways they are already poised for influence in their generation."

— Dr. Lisa Dunne, President of Chula Vista Christian University and author of six books on generational influence

THE TRUE POWER OF GIRLS

To: Jordan,
You've got the power!
—Grace Delynne

A DISCOVERY JOURNAL FOR
SELF-LOVE, CONFIDENCE, AND UNIQUENESS

GRACE DELYNNE

The True Power of Girls:
A Discovery Journal for Self-Love, Confidence, and Uniqueness

Aviva Publishing
Lake Placid, NY
518-523-1320
www.avivapubs.com

Copyright © 2022
All rights reserved, including the right to reproduce this book or any portion thereof in any form whatsoever. For information, address:

Christine Gail
christine@unleashyourrising.com

Every attempt has been made to source all quotes properly.

For additional copies or bulk purchases visit:
www.TheTruePowerofGirls.com

Editor: Tyler Tichelaar, Superior Book Productions
Publishing Coach: Christine Gail
Cover Design: Aero Gallerie
Author Photo: Brooke Preece Portrait

Library of Congress Control Number: 2022904682
Paperback ISBN: 978-1-63618-177-6

10 9 8 7 6 5 4 3 2 1
First Edition, 2022

Printed in the United States of America

Dedication

To my beloved sister Elizabeth,

my inspirational mom Christine,

and my amazing dad Chris.

Contents

Introduction	9
Chapter 1: You Can Be Inspirational	13
Chapter 2: Embracing Your Emotions	19
Chapter 3: You Are Loved	35
Chapter 4: The Power of Mindfulness and Mindset	45
Chapter 5: Girls Just Wanna Have Fun!	55
Chapter 6: Your Story	61
Chapter 7. Empower	73
Acknowledgments	81
About the Author	83

Introduction

The True Power of Girls is a book for you if you are a girl, age seven to ninety-nine! I believe girls are powerful, and this book will help you learn to find your true power and love yourself and others more. This book will also help you embrace your emotions and use your voice to live in your true power as a girl. By the time you finish reading *The True Power of Girls*, you will be inspired to discover your uniqueness, be more confident, and follow your dreams.

When I started writing this book, to be honest, I really didn't understand what true girl power really meant. I was only six years old when I started writing, and I wrote it so that maybe I would have the chance to meet Emma Watson since I've always dreamed of being an actor in movies like her and because she had a girl power book club.

Then I started to have challenges at school in first, second, and third grade. Girls who were supposed to be my friends turned out to be not so friendly. I became a different person in order to fit in. I found that the girls who were bullies had the most power, which made me feel sad and confused inside.

When I went home every day, I was a nice girl who was loved and cared for and loving to other people. I was the girl writing this book called *The True Power of Girls*. But then I felt like every time I went to school, I was a different person…mean, unfriendly, and sassy. So here I was writing this book, but really, I was struggling to understand how to have true girl power. I took lots of breaks over four years while writing this book because I was just trying to figure this out.

Then one day, in the fourth grade, I realized I was acting mean and sassy because that is the way the people around me at school acted. So I decided to try to hang out with nicer people, and it helped a little. I began to learn techniques that helped me embrace my emotions and calm my mind. I learned how to use empowering language to solve problems with friends. I also learned to ask for help and to be honest with my parents and people I trusted about the struggles I was going through. I also learned more about how I can call on God for help.

I realized that *The True Power of Girls* is the book I needed when I was in the first, second, and third grades. *The True Power of Girls* would have helped me in so many ways. If I had read this book when I was younger, I probably wouldn't have had the problems that I did back then.

I want to give this book to girls and women so they don't have to deal with the problems I dealt with. I want girls to know that they are not alone when they feel like they don't fit in or it is hard to make true friends. I want girls to read this book so they learn to love themselves and deal with these problems the right way.

If you read this book, you will be able to find your true self, learn how to embrace your emotions, and follow your dreams. Reading this book will also help you understand the concept of mindfulness and having a positive mindset. With this book, you can write down your own story. If you end up sharing your story, it can change lives! You will learn how to create habits of saying your "I am" statements to yourself every day! Once you learn how to love yourself, you will soon be able to love others like never before. As you read this book, you will grow braver, stronger, smarter, and even more inspirational.

In **Chapter 1: You Can Be Inspirational**, you will learn about women from the past and present and how you can become an inspirational woman too!

In **Chapter 2: Embracing Your Emotions**, you will find out about signal emotions and power emotions. You will also learn about how to control and embrace your emotions. If you learn how to do that, you will be treated differently because you will be treating others better. You can also create a better life with these techniques.

In **Chapter 3: You Are Loved**, you will discover how to love yourself better and how to love your neighbors better.

In **Chapter 4: The Power of Mindfulness and Mindset**, you will learn some mindfulness techniques and how to have a positive mindset to go after what you want in life.

In **Chapter 5: Girls Just Wanna Have Fun**, you will understand how to make true friends. There is a fun quiz you can do to see if the friends you have now are true friends. At the end of the chapter, you will learn five fun things to do with friends and family.

In **Chapter 6: Your Story**, I will ask you questions, some of which are fun and some personal. Don't worry. Sometimes writing down your thoughts that you don't want to tell anybody else can make you feel better about yourself. In this chapter, you will find your true self, which will help you a lot in life.

In **Chapter 7: Empower**, I will teach you how to make your own "I am" statement. You will also learn inspiring quotes and scriptures, and write down your dreams that you want to accomplish.

In this book, there will be some journaling activities. All you need to do is honestly write down the answers to the questions. Don't be worried about what other people will think if they somehow read what you wrote. It is okay just to share what is really on your mind. Trust me, the journaling will be a lot easier and help you more if you write down the truth.

In this book, I will also share stories from my past and how I worked through my past. So if you feel like you have it rough and you can't work through it, just keep reading because then you will soon learn how to work through and embrace your past too.

As you read *The True Power of Girls*, I hope you will be inspired to do the journaling exercises and want to read more. It is my wish and prayer that as you read each chapter, you will feel more loved and worthy. Visit my website: www.TheTruePowerOfGirls.com to find out how to give back to girls in need and to get more out of reading this book. I'm excited to create a True Power of Girls Movement so we can all live in our true power and support one another as stronger girls every day!

Grace DeLynne

1
You Can Be Inspirational

In this chapter, you will learn about some inspirational women from the past and the present. These women inspire me because they have done big things in life. I am also inspired by my mom and my sister. You may think about who inspires you the most. What if you could be inspirational too? The most important thing to know is that you don't have to be famous or successful to be inspirational. You can just start off by being an inspiration for friends and family, then move on to other people. Here are a few women I've learned about who inspire me the most.

One very inspirational woman is Amelia Earhart. She was the first female to fly a plane by herself all the way over the Atlantic Ocean in 1932. Even though it was a dangerous journey, she still did it and never gave up. She created the first ladies' aviation club and broke other world records for flying. Amelia was a confident girl who believed in herself. She went for her dreams even though she knew it was a big risk. If I could call her just one adjective, it would be brave.

Sacagawea was a Native American girl who lived in the early 1800s. She helped explorers translate languages to communicate with other Native Americans as they traveled to new territories through

Northern America, the Rocky Mountains, and all the way to the Pacific Ocean and back. Sacagawea was a strong girl to travel so far. And she had her son along the way. Deep down, she knew part of her purpose was to help the Lewis and Clark Expedition. If I could call her just one adjective, I would call her adventurous.

Lucille Ball was a funny girl who realized at a young age that she loved acting. When she grew up and got married, she decided to create her own TV show called *I Love Lucy*. She ended up being the first woman to own a major studio called Desilu Productions. Lucille was brave to show girls that it is a good thing to be funny so we can cherish those moments and have fun in life. She also believed that girls do not have to be so proper all the time. If I could call her just one adjective, it would be funny.

Rosa Parks was an inspirational Black woman living in the 1950s in Alabama. She was discriminated against for the color of her skin. A bus driver tried to tell her that since she was Black, she had to sit in the back of the bus. She said, "No," and for that she was sent to jail. She even lost her job over this. This began a movement to end racial discrimination. Rosa was a confident woman to take a risk like this. She knew that no matter what, she had to make things right. She knew that people have the right to stand up for themselves and they also have the right to do what other people can do, no matter their skin color. If I could call her just one adjective, it would be determined.

Meryl Streep was a young woman who loved acting. She tried out for a role in the movie *King Kong* in 1976. The producer told her she was too ugly for the part. She ended up starring in over seventy movies. She was nominated for twenty-one Academy Awards and won three. If I could call her just one adjective, it would be confident.

Tina Hovsepian was a girl who grew up in Los Angeles. She saw people living on the streets, and it made Tina feel sad. In her later years, Tina decided to study something that could help others: architecture. For her final university project, she had an idea to help the homeless. After hard work, Tina created Cardborigami. Using large pieces of cardboard, she made a folding material so it could pop up in seconds and create a little home for a homeless person. Tina was kind because she wanted to help people in need. Even though it took many months to create Cardborigami, she kept going by thinking, "When I make this home for homeless people, they will feel happy." If I could call her just one adjective, it would be kind.

Edurne Pasaban was a true mountain girl. She grew confident in herself by climbing mountains. One day, she joined a mountain club. The club was going to hike Mt. Everest, but some people were getting sick on the way, so Edurne had to walk them down to safety. Edurne was a believer. She believed in the journey and she also cared for others and did the right thing. Edurne ended up climbing Mount Everest and thirteen other mountains all the way to the top! The best adjectives to describe her are successful and empathetic.

From an early age, Smriti Mandhana dreamed of becoming a professional cricket player, but not many women played cricket in India. She watched her father and brother play, and her job was to collect the balls. As a reward, she got to hit ten balls at the end of the day. Smriti kept on practicing and finally got into the U15 (under fifteen years old) cricket team when she was just nine years old! Playing with older kids was going to be a challenge, but she knew it would make her a better player. At seventeen, she became the first Indian woman to score 200 in a one-day competition. In 2018, she was voted the best female cricket player of the year. If I could call her just one adjective, it would be strong.

Emma Watson is a great example of believing in the true power of girls because she is an advocate for equal rights for women. As an actor, she also chooses girl power roles that are very inspiring. At just eleven years old, she got cast as Hermione in *Harry Potter*. Her character Hermione is young and smart. She is determined and not afraid to speak up just like Emma Watson herself.

Emma also played Belle in *Beauty and the Beast*. Belle is strong, very smart, and loves to read. Even though people called her odd, that didn't stop her from reading more books to learn new things. She also did not judge the Beast for how he looked, but instead focused on his best qualities.

Emma also got a role as Meg in *Little Women* (the 2019 version). *Little Women* is one of the most heart-touching girl power movies. It is based on a book written long ago by Louisa May Alcott. The story is about a girl named Jo who loves to write and act with her three sisters Meg, Amy, and Beth. They have a loving family, but then Jo's father goes away to the war, her sister Beth gets diagnosed with scarlet fever, and Jo struggles with her writing. But those struggles do not stop her. They help her find new pathways to reach her dream of writing and publishing her book. Emma's role as Meg was to also show love and support for her sisters, even though they were very different. This is an important message for girls. If I were to call Emma Watson just one adjective, it would be memorable.

What's most inspiring is the author of *Little Women*. Louisa May Alcott wrote the book in 1868, and back then, women authors were very rare. Her dad created a desk for her and encouraged her to write.

She wrote the first book in ten weeks writing nonstop day and night! *Little Women* is based on Louisa's life; she just changed it a bit. Her sister did get scarlet fever and Louisa did not want to marry, just like Jo. Louisa became very successful after writing *Little Women*, and her story still lives on to this day. If I could call her one adjective, it would be impressive.

I noticed when I read more about these inspiring women that they were not only strong and determined, but they were also kind and believed in helping people. Some people may think that helping people is not a big deal. I mean it's not like you are going to win an award, but it is more Important than an award. Being loving and kind makes people around you feel good and loved!

Just think of all of these inspirational women and how they made a difference in their lifetimes. I hope these inspirational stories have inspired you to make the world a better place!

Is there something you are inspired to do or dream about doing someday? Journal about it here:

_____ _____
_____
_____
_____ _____
_____ _____

2
Embracing Your Emotions

One of the important parts about understanding your true power as a girl is embracing your emotions. You might notice sometimes your emotions can make you feel good and sometimes they can make you feel bad.

Emotions can also help you learn something about yourself. They give you an opportunity to change, use your girl power voice, or tell someone what you need and what is going on. Sometimes emotions can make you cry. It is okay to cry and tell somebody you trust about your emotions. Sometimes they can help you feel better and make things right.

In this chapter, we are going to do a lot of journaling, so go ahead and grab a pen or pencil. I will share with you about the two types of emotions: power emotions and signal emotions (some people might call them "negative" emotions). Hopefully, this chapter will give you tools to work through your signal emotions so you can feel more loved and happy.

Power Emotions
Love

Love is a very important part of life. Everyone can have love even if they do not know much about it or feel it. It is always there. You likely have someone in your life who loves you, and there is hopefully someone in your life you love very much. What is your best memory of love? (For example, one of my favorite memories of love is when my little sister was born.)

Write yours down below:

_____
_____
_____
_____

You can show someone love by doing something nice for them. For example, when I was five years old, I was getting rid of toys and wondering what I should do with them. So I asked my mom if I could give them to kids with cancer. So she called the cancer unit at Rady's Children's Hospital and asked if I could give used toys to boys and girls there. They said the children could not accept used toys because the germs on them could make them sicker. Hearing this, I felt sad because I was really excited to help these boys and girls. Then I thought of an idea: Why give used toys when we can buy new toys? So I told my mom and we went shopping for twenty boxes, ten blue for the boys and ten pink for the girls. We bought fun activities for boys and girls and packed them in the boxes. Then we realized we couldn't do it by ourselves so we called my Girl Scouts troop. The day finally came. We got to deliver all of the boxes of activities to the kids with cancer in the hospital! We didn't get to meet them, but it felt nice knowing that those activities would brighten their day. This story is an example of love because I felt love for those kids with cancer.

Write down five things you can do to be loving to yourself or someone else.

_____
_____
_____
_____
_____

Happiness

Happiness is a great feeling to have. It's when you can't stop smiling or you feel so loved inside. Happiness is a really important feeling to have because it makes you feel good and loved. What is better than that?

Here is a story of a time when I was so happy I could not stop smiling:

It was about five days before my eighth birthday. Aunt Robbie was visiting. We went to a California pizza kitchen after my gymnastics class. While I was eating, Aunt Robbie and my mom told me that they had a surprise for me. We got in the car and they drove us to a shopping center that had a Barnes & Noble in it. Since that is one of my favorite stores, I thought we were going there to get some books for me. But nope, we walked right past it. The next building was an ice cream shop so I thought we were going there. Nope. Then we came to the last building, Claire's. We walked in. I thought I was going to get something there like a bow or a plushie, so I walked around trying to figure out what I wanted. Then about five minutes later, my mom and Aunt Robbie came up to me and said, "Do you want to know the real surprise?" I said, "Sure!" and had no idea what it would be. Then they asked, "Would you like to get your ears pierced?" Of course, I said, "Yes!" When I got them pierced, it didn't even hurt. I felt so happy that I literally couldn't stop smiling!

Here is another story about happiness. This is the best day of my whole entire life so I guess you can say this is a very fun, loving, happy story.

When I was just three years old, my mom was nine months pregnant with my little sister. One morning, I woke up and walked into the hall, and there was a lady sleeping in a sleeping bag, so I ran into my parents' room and they were gone! They had told me that if my mom went into labor, a babysitter would be there for me. In my three-year-old mind, I thought that the babysitter was a bad guy. So I decided to crawl around her head to check her out closer, and I accidentally knocked down her water bottle. This made her wake up, and she told me everything that happened that night with my mom delivering my little sister in the middle of the night. So after breakfast, we went straight to the hospital, and my dad was standing right in front of it. I ran up to him, gave him a hug, and we went up the elevator. Then we stopped and I walked out of the elevator, through the hallway, feeling so excited and happy. We walked in, and there my mom was holding my little sister. Then I got to hold her for the first time. I held my sweet baby sister Elizabeth. This was my happiest moment in the world! I believe this feeling was even more than happiness. This must be joy.

EMBRACING YOUR EMOTIONS

Now I would like you to journal about your happiest moments in your life.

_____
_____
_____
_____
_____
_____

Good job!

Peace

Peace is an emotion that makes you feel good and calm. When you feel peaceful, you are aware of your surroundings. Peace is the opposite of feeling energetic and hyper. An example of a time when I felt the most peace is when I was on vacation in Sedona, Arizona. We were on a hike and ended up at a peaceful, flowing stream. I took my shoes off and waded through the water. I stacked rocks and sat on a rock in the river with my toes in the sand. I could hear the flowing water, I could see my little sister laughing, and I could feel my toes in the sand. It was just so peaceful. That moment was peaceful because I wasn't focused on the past or the future. I was focused on the present. I was focused on what was happening around me, and I felt peace in my heart.

Write down a time when you felt peaceful.

_____
_____
_____
_____
_____

Great job!

One thing about peace is that you can choose to respond with peace, even if things are crazy around you. If you feel overwhelmed, rather than reacting and being frustrated, you can think about your happiest memory or just take a deep breath and choose peace.

You can not only choose peace, but you can feel or be peaceful at any time. Now you might be wondering, "How can I get into a peaceful state?" Here is an idea. Close your eyes and imagine you are in a paradise: the beach, your house, the jungle, or wherever makes you feel safe and happy. Pretend that everyone you love or care for is with you in this beautiful paradise. When I do this exercise, my paradise is the jungle because I can hear the birds chirping, the trees swaying in the wind, and it's just so soothing in my opinion. Does being around the people you love make you happy? This makes me feel happy. Being around the people I love also makes me feel loved, protected, peaceful, and safe.

Write down three things that make you feel peaceful or that you can do anytime you feel overwhelmed.

_____
_____
_____
_____
_____

Great!

Signal Emotions

Now for the signal emotions or "negative" emotions. I would like to ask you a question. Are "negative" emotions really negative? Write down what you think and why you think that.

EMBRACING YOUR EMOTIONS 25

_____
_____
_____

Negative emotions are not actually bad. They just make you feel bad. Really they are a signal that there is something you need to be aware of about yourself, or something you need to talk about, or maybe you just need to change your perspective into love. Now, because of that, let's call them signal emotions.

Sadness

Sadness is an emotion that might make you feel not loved or lonely or maybe just hurt (physically or mentally). Before I share a story about sadness, I would like you to write down a time when you have felt sad.

_____
_____
_____
_____
_____
_____

Now it's storytime. One day, I was at school and a boy in my class yelled from across the room, "You're so ugly and fat, Grace!" This made me feel very sad! Not long before this, I had made friends with two girls who turned out to be not so nice. We would always fight about the rules of games, and they would cheat in games too. They even kicked me in the shin if I did not play what they wanted me to play. So I just kept the sadness in, and I did not tell my parents or anyone. Instead, I let it out on two nice boys in my class by correcting them in a stern voice. I told them they were not smart and that they would never pass the third grade. Then I started staying in at lunch with the other two girls in the principal's office to try to figure out why all of this was happening. All of my other friends would come up to me at lunch and ask why I was not there during lunch. I was so embarrassed that I told them lies like that my other friends and I wanted to hang out privately so we were hiding, or that I was there and I couldn't find them! I avoided telling them the truth because I did not want them to think of me as a mean girl.

I am telling you my story because everybody goes through being bullied at least once in their life, so don't feel alone if you do. And sometimes holding all that in can cause you to bully others. I learned to let all this go, and a part of that letting go was journaling.

Write about a time or times you were bullied. What did you do? How can you let it go?

_____
_____
_____
_____
_____
_____
_____
_____

So the bullying was a big struggle for me, and it made me feel very sad inside. Here I was lying, keeping things in, and even going to the principal's office! Also, a year before that, my best friend had moved away. I felt like life kept on getting harder and worse!

EMBRACING YOUR EMOTIONS

And then the pandemic hit. It all started when I just heard some things about a virus and that toilet paper was running out. Then one day at school, our teacher told us that we would be doing online learning. That was the night of the talent show, which got canceled, and I was in the talent show! Then he said it would only be for a week, but it ended up lasting so much longer! Then my birthday came along and none of my friends wanted to come over for a party. Legoland, Disneyland, the Safari Park, and all the trampoline places were all closed. All of the restaurants were closed and a ton of the food at the grocery stores was gone! Luckily, a beach condo was open, so we stayed there for a few days for my birthday. The only friend I had was my sister.

So, I would like for you to write about some struggles you have been going through in life. What has been making you feel sad?

_____
_____
_____
_____
_____
_____
_____
_____
_____
_____

Great job!

Now write about some ways that you can let the sadness go. For example, you could write down the good things that came out of it, or just pray and give it all to God. Go ahead and write down as many good things as you can think of that came out of these sad times in your life.

_____
_____
_____
_____
_____
_____
_____
_____
_____
_____

Great job!

Here is another story about sadness. Sadness can also be from losing someone you love. For me, that someone was my dog Chewy. He started getting old and sick. At first, he got so many hot spots (hot spots are like rashes for dogs and their hair falls out where the rash is. It is also itchy for the dog.), and then he got so sensitive to dog food. Then one day, he started walking weirdly like he was drunk and my dad said Chewy might be dying. He would not eat anything at all. Then all of a sudden, he started breathing very heavily like his nose and throat were clogged up. It was nighttime and I could not go to sleep. So I asked if I could sleep next to him. I did for a while, and then I kept waking up, so my mom told me to go to bed. So the next day, my parents had some news. "Chewy passed away early this morning," my dad said. I broke out crying on my mom's lap, and I did not want to go to school that day. It was two days before Halloween, so it was the day to wear my costume and get treats at school. So I decided to go to school even though I was feeling so sad inside. After school, I wrote Chewy two notes, drew him a picture, and snuggled by him and cried. We cut his hair to keep and someone came to pick him up. We prayed and cried so much knowing that Chewy's spirit was gone forever, and now I wouldn't even have his body to snuggle. To cheer us up, our dad went to our favorite café and brought me home a strawberry tart, my sister and dad a carrot cake, and my mom got chocolate cake. That is the story of how our Chewy died.

Have you ever lost someone you loved? Journal about it here.

_____
_____
_____
_____
_____

You're doing great.

Anger

Now for anger. Anger is an emotion that sometimes makes you do things that are not very nice or kind like hurting someone (physically or mentally) or doing things like slamming your door really hard and making other people angry.

Sometimes, my little sister can be annoying, like when she sings the same song over and over. I say, "Please stop!" but she keeps on going. I say in a stern voice louder, "Stop!" again, but she keeps on going! Then I yell, "Stop!" She keeps going on and on. Then my parents come in and tell her to "Stop" and she stops! When this happens, it always makes me angry. Her being annoying isn't just about singing. It's also touching me when I need my space, using my stuff, and copying or mimicking me. This makes me feel disrespected and angry.

I started doing a method that I learned in school. (This method can be used for any emotion). It is called the "I message." It goes like this:

I feel _____ (how you feel when they do it)
when you _____
_____
_____(what they did to upset you),
and I prefer that you _____
_____(what they can maybe do next time).

Then the other person could say:

I am sorry for _____
_____ and next time I will
_____
_____.

Great. Now fill in the blanks. Sometimes what I would do is write it down and give it to them. For example, if they called you a rude name you would write:

To: (the person's name)

I feel sad when you call me (put the rude name here), and I prefer that you call me by my name next time.

Also, can you fill in the blanks and give the note back to me?

I am sorry for _____
_____, and next time I will
_____
_____.

From: (your name)

You could ask your teacher at school to teach everybody the "I message" statement. Then you can say it verbally to that person. Hopefully, they will respond by saying that they are sorry or that they will not do it again. If you aren't sure how to be brave to use these "I messages," ask a friend or grownup that you trust to be with you when you say them.

Fear

Fear is an emotion that everybody has. Some people are afraid of dying, afraid of trying new things, afraid of speaking in front of people, or afraid of what other people think about them.

Here is a story about me feeling fear:

One day, my dad, my sister, and I were at the park where there was a little zip line. My sister went on it and fell. She started crying so much that she couldn't breathe and she passed out. I screamed "No!" and started crying, thinking "This is the day my sister goes to heaven." My dad started tapping on her chest and then she woke up. I was so relieved that she was alive! From then on, every time I got angry, I would at least try to think of that time because it reminds me of how much I love her.

I am telling you this because if anything bad ever happened to anybody in your life whom you love, but fight with sometimes, you can think of that moment and remember how much you love them.

Write down a story of a time when you felt fear. How did you overcome it?

_____
_____
_____
_____
_____

Here is a story of when I was fearless:

When I was eight years old I went to Manny Lopez's Serve X event. I was inspired by all of the speakers there, including my mom. I wanted to speak, so I asked my mom to ask Manny if I could speak for two minutes and she said, "Okay, I will ask him." Then I was playing with his little girl when Manny's son came up to me and said, "You're up on stage in two minutes!" I felt fearless. In fact, I was so excited that it made me feel even more excited. I didn't have anything planned. I just knew I was going to talk about *The True Power of Girls*. So I went up there and gave my speech. I felt so proud of myself afterward.

If you want to see it, ask a parent to help you go to YouTube and type in "The True Power of Girls speech by Grace DeLynne."

I am telling you this story because almost everybody is afraid of speaking in front of people because they are afraid they will mess up, or they are afraid of what other people will think of them. Just be unique, be kind, be *you*! If you are speaking or if you are in school doing a presentation, then don't care about what other people think. Think about how what you have to say may inspire someone. Think about yourself as a funny, smart, strong, beautiful girl like you are!

Write down a story of a time when you felt fearless.

_____
_____
_____
_____
_____
_____

Before I end this chapter, I'd like to remind you that when you feel signal emotions come up, remember that you can choose peace, think about something that makes you feel happy, journal, use the "I message," or just give it to God and pray. How can you embrace your emotions?

3
You Are Loved

Loving yourself is important so you can be confident in what you want to do in life. Loving yourself is also about loving others. The Bible says, "Love your neighbor as yourself." That basically means that loving others starts with loving yourself. One way to love yourself is to take care of yourself. Taking care of yourself is a very important part of life. Eating healthy foods, exercising, and doing things that make you feel peaceful and happy is taking care of yourself. This affects you now and when you get older.

Another way of loving yourself is by saying positive things about yourself. For example, "I am strong, I am loved, I am amazing, I am beautiful." These affirmations help me, and they can help you feel better. What you speak out loud can either cause life or death over your life. When you speak something, it puts it out into the universe. So if you keep on saying the same thing, you will start believing it and it can come true. This is why it is so important to speak good things about yourself.

Loving yourself doesn't mean that you just care about yourself and not others. Loving yourself means that it starts with loving yourself, and then you can care for and love others the same.

Another way of loving yourself is accepting your flaws and your imperfections. One day at school, my friend and I were playing in the bathroom with face paint. She turned to me and said, "I'm glad I don't have your face. It's ugly." This made me feel sad for a little bit. I thought I got over it, but later, I think I probably just kept it in and left it there. I also had people at school make fun of my freckles. One time they asked me, "Why do you have polka dots on your face?" I said back to them, "Well, they aren't polka dots. They are freckles, and I think polka dots are very fashionable." That was a good comeback to them, but I think inside it hurt my heart to hear what they said because after that I began hating my freckles. I finally cried to my mom about them, and she helped me realize that the freckles made me unique and more beautiful. Believing that they are actually kisses from angels helped too.

What are some things that have made you feel self-conscious about yourself that you can see now in a different way and love about yourself?

_____
_____
_____
_____
_____

Sometimes, things happen in your life that can keep you from fully loving yourself. Here is a story of something that was bothering me and started to affect how I treated other people.

Over a year ago, I noticed I was getting annoyed with my sister more easily. One day, I was so mad at her that I yanked her arm and she started crying. I felt bad, but my anger had taken over, so I went into my room. I could not understand why I was getting so annoyed so easily. After saying I was sorry to my sister, I was brave enough to ask my mom to do breakthrough work on me. Breakthrough work is when you find the root cause of your signal emotion and sometimes your root cause is from generations ago! I had done breakthrough work a few times before, and I did not like it at first! This time I felt like I really needed it. My root cause turned out to be guilt from bullying a little boy in school. This is how it all happened….

One day at school, a teacher said I had to have a meeting with the principal. When I went into the room, the two girls and one boy who had bullied me were in the room too. I took a seat and then the principal said, "Someone is absent in your class because of you guys bullying him, mostly you, Grace. In fact, you have been mean in kindergarten, first grade, second grade, and now third grade. You are mean, mean, mean!"

I almost ran out of the room crying. I was tempted to, but I never did. I just kept it all inside. The principal and teachers had not seen how these kids had bullied me, and now the only way I felt I could fit in at this school was to make fun of people too. But I knew I was wrong. That weekend, I couldn't stop thinking about how guilty I was. "I actually could have been nice to this boy," I would think every night.

I gave him a note that said, "I am sorry. I hope we can be friends." I gave it to him after lunch. After that, our teacher taught us about the pandemic for the first time, and he said there would be a lockdown for a week so we had to gather all of our stuff and go home. (Although, he didn't know it was going to be more than a year.) School got out early, and I have never heard from the boy I bullied since. I never knew what he felt about the note, and I kept all of that inside.

So that was my root cause of guilt. Carrying this guilt was causing me to be less patient with my sister. So with a little help from my mom, God, Jesus, and the Holy Spirit, my guilt went away. My mom walked me through a visualization, and Jesus was there. He talked to me for the first time ever. This made me feel so loved and happy! The talk with Jesus was so amazing for me because it was the first time he talked to me. He said, "Grace, I will always be with you, holding your hand. Even though there will be mountains you climb and rivers you cross in life, I will always be by your side. I will talk to the boy you bullied, and tell him you are sorry. God has a plan for you, and you are on the right path. Your book is going to change lives. Just keep on being yourself and sharing about God. I love you."

That is what he said. I will never forget it.

I still feel like I want to say sorry in person to this boy and tell him I did not mean any of what I said, but neither of us go to that school anymore. I still think we could have been really good friends, but sometimes when sadness, fear, or anger takes over, you can turn into a bully like I used to be. Now thanks to that breakthrough work and God and Jesus, I am healed and I've never felt better!

You know the saying, "Everything happens for a reason"? If it were not for a fight with my sister, I might have never been healed of the guilt I had been carrying for over a year! I was able to love myself again because I felt loved by God.

By the way, you may never have had Jesus speak to you, and that is okay. It is something that unexpectedly happened in the breakthrough, and I understand maybe it does not make sense to some people. What you can think about is that sometimes you can receive an answer in a dream, or through someone else telling you something, or maybe it almost sounds like a little whisper in your ear that could have been God or Jesus giving you an answer to something, or a knowing that you have like your intuition. One thing you can try is to close your eyes right here, right now and say out loud or in your head, "God or Jesus, what do you want to say to me?" Ask them whatever question is on your heart to ask like: "What is my purpose and how can I pursue it?" Ask them whatever else you want to ask, or just talk to them.

How do you feel? Did you get an answer? If not, that is okay. Some people do not get an answer from God until they are a grown-up. That does not mean that God or Jesus does not love you. I think it might take practice. But if Jesus did talk to you just now or any time before this, write it down here. Or if you have ever received an answer to a question you asked when you closed your eyes, write it down here:

_____
_____
_____   _____
_____   _____
_____

Another way to connect with and feel loved by God is to read the Bible.

Here are my top three favorite scriptures…

"God is love." 1 John 1:8

"God is within her, she will not fall." Psalms 46:5

"'For I know the plans I have for you,' declares the Lord, 'plans to prosper you and not harm you, plans to give you hope and a future.'" Jeremiah 29:11

What do these scriptures mean to you?

_____
_____
_____

If you read the Bible already, write down your favorite scripture here, or write your favorite scripture that I said.

_____
_____
_____

Now that we have talked about how you can let go of things that cause you to be hard on yourself, it is time to talk about more ways to love yourself physically and mentally.

Now I would like for you to look in a mirror and write down what you see physically.

_____
_____
_____

Now write down what you see mentally.

_____
_____
_____

Look over what you wrote and now answer this question:

Do you think good things or bad things about yourself?

_____

If you think good things, that is great! If you do not think good things about yourself, then what do you not like about yourself? Write it here:

_____

How can you think differently about what you wrote so that you can instead like this about yourself?

_____
_____
_____

I used to be self-conscious about the hair on my arms and legs. If I were around my best friends, then I did not mind because they would never judge me. But before, when I was in class at school or at church, I used to put my arms behind me so that they would not show, and if I were wearing a skirt, shorts, or a dress, I would sit on my knees. Now I do not care what other people think of me. All I care about is what I think of myself.

The best way to think better about yourself is to start believing in yourself with your words. Here is a story of how your words are very important.

I was at gymnastic camp one day and there was a three-year-old girl there named Ryan. She was practicing cartwheels and she fell once and said, "I can't do it! I lost my cartwheel!" I said to her, "Try again!" She said, "Fine…but I can't do it." She tried again and then fell, again.

Then I said, "Let's take a break from cartwheels and go into storytime." So I sat her down and told her this story:

"Once upon a time there was a girl named Ryan who lost her cartwheel and she couldn't find it anywhere! Then Ryan's coach told her that if she said: 'I can do a cartwheel' and tried to do one, she would land it. So Ryan tried a cartwheel and landed on her feet!"

After I told Ryan that story, she stood up and said, "I am Ryan and I can do a cartwheel." Then she stood up, ran, and did a cartwheel! She got so excited and jumped up and down, saying, "I can do a cartwheel!" From then on, she landed all of her cartwheels except for one. She fell on the landing, but when she fell, she said, "Get back up again!" She got back up and kept landing the cartwheels one after another.

I love the story because it reminds me of how powerful your words can be.

Now write an "I can" or "I am" statement about yourself and say it out loud or whisper it to yourself.

_____

If you like, go ahead and write more!

_____
_____
_____

Now back to the self-conscious thing. Write down who you feel most self-conscious around.

_____

If it is a bully, I just want you to know that the only reason people bully other people is because they are hurting inside themselves. They may be jealous of something about you. Perhaps because of how pretty you are. Remember that everybody is pretty in their own way. Or maybe it is because you are different. It is a good thing if you are different! Also, if you think that nobody loves you, say this out loud: "God loves me!"

Now, if it is a boy you feel self-conscious around, then I get it. A boy you like can sometimes make you think about what he thinks about you. It can be confusing sometimes. This might make you try to cover up what you are self-conscious about or make you act differently. Remember to just be yourself!

If you start acting this way around the so-called "popular kids" just to fit in, I think that is not right. I know this from my own life. If you cannot be yourself around friends, then they might not be your true friends anyway. You should act like yourself around everyone! You are unique and beautiful in your own way. Besides, God loves you and he will never stop loving you because he created you perfect just the way you are. If everybody looked and acted the same, the world would be so boring! So you have the right to spice things up a bit and be your own amazing self!

Just remember you are loved.

4
The Power of Mindfulness and Mindset

There are two things that are super-important if you want to live in your true power as a girl. They are mindfulness and mindset. They are alike in some ways because they both involve your mind. Mindfulness is a strategy that helps your mind calm down. Mindset is also very important because it helps you think better things about yourself so you can do what you love to do. They both make you feel good and are really great things to have in your life.

Mindfulness

Mindfulness can be done anywhere, anytime, no matter what is going on. You do not have to sit down and close your eyes to do mindfulness, although sometimes you can. Mindfulness is basically being in the present moment, not focusing on the past or the future, and not having a movie in your brain all the time. Mindfulness is focusing on what is around you, listening to your surroundings, smelling the air, breathing in and out, and using your senses!

Clearing your brain of all the busy thoughts is another great way to do mindfulness! If you have trouble going to sleep, like me, you can practice mindfulness before you go to bed or while you are in bed. This is what I do when I am in bed. I lay down with my hands at my sides and my palms facing up. I curl my toes, and then I squeeze my legs, then my stomach, hands, and shoulders, until my whole body is tightened up. Then one by one I relax each part of my body. Did you know that calming down your mind helps you connect to your heart more too?

Mindfulness is also a very powerful strategy to use when you are mad, angry, sad, upset, or even when you are happy. Below are more mindfulness strategies.

Sit in a comfortable spot and do these thingamabobs.

I like to call mindfulness techniques thingamabobs!

1. Find a comfortable spot. Sit or lay there and just practice breathing slowly in and out. If you would like, you can also grab a squishy or a stuffed animal and hold it in your hands. So when you breathe in, you squish the squishy or stuffed animal, and when you breathe out, relax your hands.

2. Finger breaths are also a good calm down strategy. Here is how they work. Put your hand in the air. Trace your hand with your pointer finger from your other hand. When your pointer finger traces up your finger, breathe in, and when your pointer finger traces down your finger, breathe out.

3. Elevator breath is another helpful way of calming your mind down. Here is how it works. Put your arm out with your palm facing up. As you breathe in, reach your hand up with your palm still facing up. As you breathe out, let your hand fall to its original spot.

THE POWER OF MINDFULNESS AND MINDSET

4. Square breath is a great way to make your mind peaceful inside. Here is how it works. Make an invisible square in the air using your finger. Reach your hand out. Stick your pointer finger out. As your pointer finger makes its way up, breathe in. Next, hold it for a second. Then drag your finger to the right while breathing out. Hold it again at the corner. Then breathe back in again as you drag your finger down. Finally, hold again. Then as your finger slides right to its original spot, breathe out again.

5. Flower breath is another way for your mind to be peaceful. Here is how it works. Put your hands in a prayer position. Keep your fingertips touching and then move apart the inside of your hands as if you were holding an invisible ball. Then as you breathe in, open up your fingers and reach your hands up to the sky. Then as you breathe out, make your hands go back to their original position.

What is your favorite mindfulness technique, and would you like to try this one time per day?

Favorite mindfulness technique: _____

I will try mindfulness one time per day. (Circle one)   Yes   No

Learning About the Brain

So you may be wondering, *How do these techniques calm down my mind?* It helps to understand about the parts of the brain that are not calm. I had fun researching this so I can better understand.

Dan Siegal is a brain expert who talks about "flipped lid." "Flipped lid" is when the signal emotion part of your brain takes control over everything. The part of your brain where the signal emotions are is called the amygdala or some people call it the "caveman brain."

Try this: Make a fist with your thumb tucked in. The thumb would be the caveman part of your brain and your fingers would be the power part of your brain, which is also called the frontal lobe. So your fingers are on top of the thumb, and when you look at this, imagine it is your brain.

Your fingers are the peaceful zone, but if somebody gets on your nerves, the calming and peaceful zone disappears as those fingers flip up to reveal your thumb. Imagine your thumb as the angry, frustrated, controlling part of your brain.

When you get mad, angry, frustrated, or afraid, the signal emotion part of your brain is shown and the power part of your brain has its lid flipped up. That is why they call it "flipped lid." Now, of course, your brain does not actually do this, but this is an exercise to understand how the brain works.

What I learned is that we can show to our teacher or our family that we have a "flipped lid," or are feeling signal emotions, by showing that signal of your fingers up in the air with the thumb showing. This lets them know you may need some help calming down or you need to take a break.

So whenever you feel like you have a "flipped lid," use one of the mindfulness strategies above. They will help you become more aware of your feelings and calm yourself down.

I Messages

"I messages" are also a helpful way to work things out when you are mad, angry, or frustrated. We already talked about these in Chapter 2: Embracing Your Emotions. If you have more "I messages" you would like to fill out, go ahead and write them below. If not, you can keep on reading and not do the activity again.

Remember if something is bothering you, say this to the person.

(Fill in the blanks below by using something that bothers you that you have not solved yet).

I feel _____ (*how you feel when they do it*)

when you _____

_____ (*what they did to upset you*),

and I prefer that you _____

_____

(*what they can maybe do next time*).

Now that you know what to do, pause reading and do it now. If they are not there with you, maybe you can call them. It is probably better to say it in person to them the next time you see them. Write more down if you would like to practice more!

I feel _____ when you _____

_____

and I prefer that you _____

_____

_____

I feel _____ when you _____
_____
and I prefer that you _____
_____
_____.

Now how did that feel? Put a checkmark next to the feelings you felt when you filled in the blanks. Then share why below. Or if there are other feelings that you felt, you can also write about them below.

Happy ( ) Sad ( ) Good ( )
Nervous ( ) Scared ( ) Thankful ( )

_____
_____
_____

So, how do "I messages" help you use mindfulness? Well, to create the message, you have to really pay attention to the words you are using. You are being mindful of the power of your words to ask for what you need. Mindfulness can help you create the best "I messages" too.

Here is a little story of me using mindfulness. I was jumping on the trampoline one day practicing a back handspring and back tuck. I kept on landing wrong and was scared I would get hurt. I kept trying, and I kept failing. This made me more and more frustrated. It got to the point where I was out of breath and my legs were tired, so I sat down and practiced some mindfulness techniques. When I did, good thoughts came over me like: "You can do this. I know you can," "It takes time," "You will get there," and "No matter what, you can do it!" All of these words came into me until there was a smile on my face. So I got up and tried again with all of these words in my head. With a smile on my face, I tried it and I didn't land it again. So, I tried again, but first, I asked myself, "What am I doing wrong?" The answer was I didn't have that much momentum, so I tried again, jumping higher and…I landed it! So, just remember if you are trying something over and over again, use mindfulness and think of messages to yourself like I did, and one day you will do it!

This leads us to the topic of mindset.

Mindset

Sometimes, your thoughts can mess you up because your inner critic starts saying things like, "You can't do it," "You're not loved," "You're weird," "You're not smart," or "You're not good enough." Mindfulness can help you calm down your mind so you can focus on what you want to do.

Mindset is where you set your mind to what you are going to do and it helps you actually do it.

It helps to delete out all of your signal emotion thoughts like "You are not enough" and "You cannot do It." Just say out loud, "Cancel!" to delete them out.

Mindset is also saying motivational things to yourself so you can do what you want to do. So next time you come across some thoughts that do not make you feel good, remember about your mindset and set your mind to whatever helps you feel good about yourself.

Here is a story of how I used a positive mindset to focus on my dreams.

Once I got an opportunity to go to a 100X Conference hosted by Pedro and Suzette Adeo. On the first day, I met Pedro and asked him if I could meet Les Brown since I knew he was going to be there. Les

Brown is the #1 Motivational Speaker in the world. Pedro told me that Les would be there and if I stuck around, I would likely meet him since he was going to visit the kids in the NextGen 100x Kids Conference. From then on, I started to have the mindset to meet Les Brown.

We were worried we might miss him though, because we had to go back to San Diego that night and then come back to Los Angeles the next day. It was a two-hour drive back, and we barely made it in time to meet him. I kept telling myself that we were going to make it! And we did, just a little bit of time before he walked in.

It took a positive mindset for me to talk to Les and take a picture with him. He said he would endorse my book without me even asking him, which is a great blessing for me because I wasn't sure if he would want to endorse it. I was very relieved and grateful that he wanted to endorse *The True Power of Girls*! I got to hear Les give his motivational speech and I learned some speaking tips from him. This also gave me a more positive mindset around speaking on stage.

The next day, I heard that some of the kids from the 100X NextGen Kids Conference would be able to speak on stage and tell everybody in the grownup 100X Conference what they learned about in the past two days. I was very excited, so I planned out what I would say if I got to speak on stage. I decided to promote my book and tell everybody how they could contact me if they wanted me to speak on their stage or be in one of their movies. I also planned to tell them where they could buy my book. I was very excited.

A couple of hours later, I found out I would be speaking on stage. I brought my demo book, which was just my cover wrapped around another book since my book was still in editing. I was so excited to share with everyone what I had learned and about my book.

As I was waiting backstage, a huge feeling of nervousness came over me as I practiced what I would say and I kept messing up. I was super-scared that I would mess up and embarrass myself in front of all those people. But then I decided to use mindfulness and a positive mindset to feel more confident and calm. The mindfulness techniques helped calm me down. Then I used mindset so I could set my mind and tell myself that I was going to do a great job speaking in front of all of those people and that people were going to love my book. Using these techniques really helped me in that time. As I walked on stage, my heart would not stop beating. I said a little prayer and I was so excited! Then I got this huge smile plastered over my face as the teacher gave me the microphone. I started speaking about the speaking tips I had learned from Les, and then I shared about my book. When I was done with my one-minute speech, Pedro Adeo talked to me on stage using the microphone! He asked me where he could find my book. I told him my website was www.TheTruePowerOfGirls.com. Then he said he was going to buy 100 copies of my book! I was so excited. Then he said I could speak on his stage at his next 100X event! I could not believe this had all happened. The audience cheered me on when I walked off stage. I was so grateful and excited. People came up to me afterward asking again where they could find my book. I got so many book sales, and this made me feel so proud of myself. I know that if it weren't for mindfulness and mindset, my mind would have totally gone blank and I would have been too shy to share about my book.

How can you use mindfulness and mindset when you feel nervous just like I did?

_____
_____
_____

You might be thinking that mindfulness and mindset are both hard because you always have so much going on in life and in your head. You might not have a very positive mind, so it may feel very hard to use them. It might also be hard to do mindfulness because you are always thinking of the past or the future and you are never really in the present. But trust me—with practice, you can have a positive mindset and practice mindfulness all the time. I said with practice, because to be honest with you, I am still working on mindfulness and mindset so it is okay if you do not have the hang of it quite yet.

5
Girls Just Wanna Have Fun!

In this chapter, we will have a ton of fun! We will talk about friends and things you love to do, and at the end, I will give you five fun things to do with your friends and family!

Friends are so fun to have because they will always have your back if they are good friends, and it is fun to hang out with them at school or at your house. Sometimes, it is hard to find good friends, and that is why at most schools there is a lot of drama over who is friends with who. When you are friends with popular kids, you are cool, but if you are friends with unpopular or nerdy kids, people think you are not cool. This is a problem at most schools, and I know a lot of girls who experience this problem. That is why you should be grateful for the good friends you have and always treat them nicely.

Who are your best friends? What kinds of qualities do they have?

My Friends	Qualities

One way to choose the right friends is to watch how they treat other people. Do they treat people nicely? Do they talk badly about other people or gossip? Do they bully other people? Make sure you are choosing your friends not by what they look like and their popularity, but by how they are inside and how they act toward you and others.

Here is a quiz to find out if your friends are good friends or bad friends. Before you start, grab a piece of paper and a pen. Write down all of your friends' names and write your answers to each of the questions below. Then find out who are your good friends and who are your not-so-good friends.

When you have a brand-new outfit and you show it to your friends do they:

    A. Compliment you and say, "That is so cute!"

    B. Ignore it. They do not care about fashion or you.

    C. Say, "That is so out of style. Is it a hand-me-down from your grandma?"

When you share with your friends that you just hit 500 subscribers on YouTube and you're so excited, do they say:

    A. "Congratulations! OMG that is so cool! I am friends with a famous person!"

    B. "Thanks for bragging. I mean honestly, give it a break!"

    C. "You think that's a lot? I have over a million subscribers. That's like zero compared to me."

When they find out that you think a boy is cute, do they:

    A. Promise to keep it a secret…and they actually do.

    B. Tell everyone.

    C. Tell you how weird and dorky he is, then post it online.

When you let your friend borrow something, do they:

- A. Give it back right away.
- B. Keep on forgetting to give it back so much you think they are keeping it on purpose.
- C. Say, "I did not borrow that! Besides that is so lame. Why would I borrow it!

When you drop your lunch, do your friends:

- A. Help you clean it up, then give you some of their lunch.
- B. Ignore it.
- C. Laugh and then take a picture and post it to embarrass you.

When you and your friend are partners in math and you keep asking your partner for help on a math problem, do they:

- A. Act patient with you and help you.
- B. Ignore you and tell you to ask the teacher.
- C. Make fun of you because you need help.

If you answered mostly A's:

You have a great friend by your side! They are kind, respectful, and very supportive. You love being their friend and you can talk to them about anything. Make sure you are kind, respectful, and supportive of them! These are great friends to keep!

If you answered mostly B's:

Your friend doesn't really care about being your friend or not. They might be jealous of you. One day they are nice and the next they are not so nice. If you have a friend like this, talk to them about it. Say, "Hey, some days you are nice and other days you are not. I would like to talk about this more so that we can be good friends every day, not just some days."

If you answered mostly C's:

Your friend is not nice at all and you feel hurt when they say things that are rude. If you have a friend like this, you should definitely stop hanging out with them. Like the saying goes: "You become who you hang out with." You wouldn't want to become a bully like they are. Trust me, I learned that the hard way.

Now for the fun part!

Are you having enough fun in life? If you feel like you're not, ask your parents how you can have more fun in your family and with your friends. You can also have fun by yourself doing things that you love.

Write down some fun things you would love to do by yourself.

_____
_____
_____
_____

Write down some fun things you would love to do with your family.

_____
_____
_____
_____

Write down some fun things you would love to do with your friends.

_____
_____
_____
_____

Now for even more fun!

Here are five things to do with your friends or family:

1. **Skeleton in the Closet.** This is a great game to get to know each other better. Here is how you play: It is pretty easy actually. Just go around and say your deepest secret. (I would recommend playing this with your best friend whom you can tell anything to.)

2. **Would You Rather.** Go into your kitchen cabinets or refrigerator and find your least favorite foods. Be sure to ask your parents' permission first. Put the items all together on the table. Then with each item ask: "Would you rather eat (pick one of the gross foods) or (pick another gross food)?" Then whichever one they choose, they have to eat one or two bites! Remember to get water and napkins before you start!

3. **Music Video.** Do you like music videos? Well this is for you! Pick your favorite song and get all dressed up. Grab some props and make up a dance. If you like, grab a camera and create your own music video!

4. **Creative Cooking.** Do you like cooking? Even if you don't, let's make it fun! Buy your favorite foods or gather the ones you have at home. Get creative and make a yummy (or yucky) combination! If you want, make a mountain or shape out of your creation. Name your combination and find some judges (family or friends) to rate it. Have your judges try your combination and rate it one out of ten. Remember, it is not about winning. It is about having fun!

5. **Dress Up Act.** Get your camera out and some funny, cool, or fancy clothes. Practice your fashion model walk, facial expressions, and poses in the mirror. Then gather your friends and family. Some are in the show and some are watching. Have fun pretending. Whatever you are wearing, pretend like you are that character. For instance, I could dress up like the queen wearing a fancy dress and crown, and my friend or sibling could dress up like a rapper with a gold necklace and parachute pants. We could act like the rapper worked at a coffee shop and the queen was ordering. I would have an English accent and be very specific with my order. The rapper would be talking loud, rapping, and get the order wrong ten times! The sillier you are with your dress-up act, the more fun this will be!

I hope this chapter was fun for you. If you like, tag me and hashtag #thetruepowerofgirls in a picture of yourself having fun doing what you love or with your family or friends. Ask your family and friends for more ideas on how to have more fun together. I would love to see the fun you are having! Be creative and find new friends (great friends) who want to have fun too!

6
Your Story

An important part of the true power of girls is knowing that your story is powerful. Everything that has ever happened in your life is for a purpose…to help you find your true power as a girl. I learned so much about myself and my story just by writing this book and being honest with myself no matter what. This chapter is all about your story. This is a journaling activity chapter where you can be yourself, write down your feelings, and write your story.

Hi! My name is _____.

I am _____ years old.

My favorite color is _____.

I have ___ ___ siblings.

My favorite subject in school is:

_____ _____

My favorite thing to do is:

_____

_____ _____

I want to be a/an _____

when I am older and I might also be interested in being a/an ____

_____.

My favorite food is:

_____

My favorite movie or TV show is:

_____

_____

My top three wishes are:

_____

_____

_____

My favorite song is:

_____

Something personal about me is:

_____

_____

_____

My biggest fears are:

_____

_____

_____

YOUR STORY

Write out your vision of your "dream life":

_____
_____
_____
_____
_____
_____
_____

Write down five things about yourself that make you proud:

_____
_____
_____
_____
_____

Write three things that you like about your appearance:

_____
_____
_____

Who are you most grateful to have in your life:

_____
_____

I am happiest when:

_____
_____
_____

I wish girls weren't expected to:

_____
_____
_____
_____

If I were not afraid of anything, I would:

_____
_____
_____
_____
_____

I am self-conscious about:

_____
_____
_____

My favorite memory is:

_____
_____
_____
_____
_____

My worst memory is:

_____
_____
_____
_____
_____

YOUR STORY

Thinking about this makes me feel yucky inside:

_____
_____
_____

Thinking about this makes me feel good inside:

_____
_____
_____

My hero is:

_____

My best friend is:

_____

I love to:

_____

I am unique because:

_____

The biggest challenge in my life right now is:

_____
_____
_____

This is so challenging because:

_____
_____
_____
_____
_____
_____
_____

I feel most safe and loved when:

_____
_____
_____

No matter how hard your day is going, what is the number one thing that will make it better?

_____
_____
_____

I am afraid that if people knew _____
_____

about me, I would lose my friends and lose my love from people.

Write down the words you really need to hear right now and why:

_____
_____
_____
_____
_____

YOUR STORY

If I didn't have fear, sadness, or anger, then I would have never learned:

_____
_____
_____
_____
_____

If you could go back in time to when you were younger (choose any age you like), what would you say to yourself and how would that change your life?

_____
_____
_____
_____
_____
_____

Write a note to your future self on a separate piece of paper. Decide how old you will be in the future when you read it again. Make it about ten lines long. Start with "Dear future self…." End it with "Love, (your name)." Put the letter in a shoebox. Tape it up really well all over, and put a note on it not to open it until a certain date. Lastly, remember to find it and read it when you are that old!

If you had to move to the other side of the world, what would you want people to remember about you?

_____
_____
_____
_____
_____

If you could change one thing about yourself, what would it be?

_____
_____

Why do you want to change that?

_____
_____
_____

Have people made fun of this thing you want to change before?

_____
_____

What are you ready to let go of?

_____
_____

What do you want more of in your life?

_____

What are your top three goals you want to achieve by the end of the year?

_____
_____
_____

Why do you want to achieve these goals?

_____
_____
_____

YOUR STORY

Now let's write about who you are inside but in a fun way by using your name as an acronym. For instance, my name is Grace, so I would write…

Graceful

Respectful

Adventurous

Caring

Exciting

Now it is your turn to make an acronym out of your name with positive adjectives! If you would like some ideas for adjectives, here are some to use…or make up your own!

A is for Adventurous, Amusing, and Amazing.

B is for Beautiful, Brave, and Bright (happy and positive).

C is for Caring, Cheerful, Compassionate, Courageous, and Cool.

D is for Daring, Determined, and Dynamic.

E is for Enchanting, Energetic, Enthusiastic, and Exciting.

F is for Fierce, Fearless, Faithful, and Fascinating.

G is for Generous, Giving, Girly, Great, and Graceful.

H is for Hard-Working, Helpful, Humble, and Humorous.

I is for Intelligent and Intuitive.

J is for Joyful, Joyous, Jolly, and Jumpy.

K is for Kind.

L is for Likeable, Lively, Loving, and Loyal.

M is for Magnificent, Magnetic, and Memorable.

N is for Nice and Non-Judgmental.

O is for Observant, Organized, and Optimistic.

P is for Passionate, Patient, Peaceful, Polite, Playful, Powerful, and Persistent.

Q is for Quick-Witted and Quiet.

R is for Reliable, Resilient, Relentless, Responsible, and Respectful.

S is for Self-Disciplined, Sincere, Sophisticated, and Sympathetic.

T is for Trustworthy, Thriving, and Trusting.

U is for Understanding, Understandable, Unique, and Unassuming.

V is for Versatile, Vibrant, Victorious, and Venturous.

W is for Wise, Wonderful, and Well-Read.

X is for Xenial (being nice or friendly).

Y is for Young and Youthful.

Z is for Zealous (great energy or enthusiasm).

Write down an acronym of your name. If you'd like, you can write it on a big piece of paper and hang it on your wall or a little piece of paper and put it on your mirror.

Great job! This is a great way to express yourself as a person! You can also write acronyms of your friends' and family's names to give to them. Make sure the words you put in the acronym are positive and kind to that person. Remember, words have power!

Now I would like for you to look in a mirror and write down what you see physically.

_____

_____

Now what do you see mentally?

_____
_____

Look over what you wrote, and based on it, I would like you to answer this question: Do you love yourself?

_____

If you do, that is great! If you answered "maybe" or anything other than "yes," then what do you not like about yourself?

_____
_____

How can you turn around what you do not like about yourself so that you love that about yourself instead?

_____
_____

What do you think God would say about all the things he loves about you?

_____
_____
_____
_____
_____

Now it is time to write down your story. Include something that happened in your life that made you change in a good way or that helped you learn an important lesson about yourself or about life. This thing helped you find your true power as a girl. Write it in a way so if someone were to read it, they would feel inspired or happy inside.

Did you enjoy writing your story? Journaling about your stories and what is going on in your life is a great way to find your true girl power. Remember, your story is powerful, and so are you!

7
Empower

This last chapter is all about empowering yourself. It is the final step to living in your true girl power! We will talk about affirmations and following your dreams, and I will share with you my girl power mission.

Here is an inspirational quote to get you motivated for this chapter…

"Believe you can, and you're halfway there."
— Theodore Roosevelt

(Say this 3 times over and over again in the mirror.)

For this activity, I would like you to make an "I am" statement. An "I am" statement is an affirmation of all of your best qualities! For instance, mine is: "I am a strong, athletic, compassionate leader!"

Below, circle three positive adjectives that best describe you. If there are any words not listed here, write your own.

Athletic Strong Beautiful Smart Compassionate Kind Loving Empathetic Funny Fun Unique Caring Adventurous Brave

Now circle one noun that best describes you or write your own.

Girl Leader Power Girl Kingdom Builder World Changer

Next, write down your "I am" statement. It will be three adjectives and one noun and start with the words, "I am." For example, my "I am" statement is: "I am a strong, smart, compassionate leader!"

I am _____

_____!

Great job! Now get some markers and a piece of paper or a large poster. Write your "I am" statement with your favorite colors! Let the creativity begin!

After you make your "I am" statement, if it is on a small piece of paper, tape it to your mirror in the bathroom or by your bed. If it is a big sheet of poster board, hang it up on your wall in your room.

Making your "I am" statement and saying it every day is a great way to practice a positive mindset. In fact, did you know that a verse in the Bible says that God is the great "I am" (Genesis 17:1)? So when you say, "I am" and then your affirmation, you are really connecting to God and to the power of how you were created.

Now with your "I am" statement, you can empower yourself to be your own unique self and go after your dreams!

Now, I would like you to write down a time when you tried to do something over and over again and you just couldn't do it. Journal about it and then write whether you accomplished it or not.

_____

_____

_____

_____

EMPOWER 75

Great job! Now if you did accomplish it, how did it make you feel?

_____
_____
_____

If you still have not accomplished this dream, write down how you can accomplish it. Maybe all you have to do is notice your mistakes and correct them. Maybe it just takes having a positive mindset and then creating a plan to do it!

_____
_____   _____
    _____
_____
_____
_____

Now write out what your dream or goal is and a step-by-step plan on how you will accomplish it. If you need help, ask a parent or someone who can help you accomplish it.

_____
_____
_____ _____
_____ _
_____
_____

So you may be thinking this is exciting and all, but it can be really hard to go after big things. Sometimes, it can be really hard even to do just one small thing. Just try your best and start with the one small thing.

For instance, when I was acting in theater, I started out getting small parts. I did the best I could with those small parts, and I had so much fun. When I was in kindergarten, we had a school production with kids of all ages in it. It was called *How the Grinch Stole Christmas*. I auditioned for the part of Cindy Lou Who, but because I was too young, the director couldn't cast me as Cindy Lou Who. Instead, she wrote in another part for me called Cute Little Who. I was so excited that I got this little part, and I had so much fun.

As I grew older, I got to be in bigger plays, but since I was still so young, I still got little parts. I keep believing that as I have fun and do my best, someday my bigger dream to be in movies will happen!

One of the last roles I was in was at our church Awaken. They put on a musical production every Christmas called *Twisted*. I was so excited to audition, and I got in! *Twisted* is a play written by Jurgen Matthesius and it is the story of how Scrooge became Scrooge. While we were practicing the scenes, the director, Anika Aguirre, looked me in the eyes and said, "Grace, do you know the song 'Just Like Heaven'?" I said, "Yes I do." She said, "Well, you got the solo for the song." I was so excited and it all happened so quickly! I had sent in my singing audition, so once she met me, she knew I was right for that part and I got it. All of those little parts I had in the past led me to this bigger part where I actually had to wear a microphone and sing the very last song of the show. It was so amazing to be a part of something so big and important.

I believe that those are the kinds of things that happen when you live in your true power. Just keep going after your little dreams and they will lead to the bigger ones!

Here are some motivational quotes to help you keep going:

*"You were put on this earth to achieve your greatest self,
to live your purpose, and to do it courageously."*
— Steve Marabou

"The most effective way to do it, is to do it."
— Amelia Earhart

"Courage is grace under pressure."
— Ernest Hemingway

"You were given this life because you are strong enough to live it."
— Ain Eineziz

"Other people's opinion of you does not have to become your reality."
— Les Brown

"Beauty is not about something as temporary as looking picture-perfect, makeup, or clothes. Beauty is about being yourself to be comfortable in your perfect imperfection!"
— Shadab Nabi

"When a woman stands up for herself, she stands up for all women."
— Maya Angelou

"Fear cannot be trusted."
— Queen Elsa

*"Sometimes you can't see what you're learning
until you come out on the other side."*
— Wonder Woman

"Love one another, as I have loved you."
— Jesus Christ

Here is a quote I created. Write it on a piece of paper and put it on your mirror.

Mirror, mirror, on the wall.
Just keep standing straight and tall.
Setting goals and achieving them.
And guess what?
I believe in them!

(Find more of my quotes on my Instagram account @grace_delynne.)

I hope you have enjoyed reading this book and learning how to love yourself, believe in yourself, and find the power in your unique story. I wrote this book because I want girls like you to discover your uniqueness and true purpose in life. I do not want you to struggle like I did to understand your emotions.

Now with these tools, you can embrace your emotions and practice having a positive mindset. I want you to know that you can empower yourself and even ask God for help, no matter what everyone else is saying.

I believe that *The True Power of Girls* will help you remember that you are loved. I wish for every girl and woman to always stay true to her heart and to be herself. I believe if we can learn to ask for help when we need it, then we can be more powerful as girls.

If these amazing techniques have helped you, I hope you will tell others about *The True Power of Girls*. It is my personal mission to help underprivileged girls and girls coming out of human trafficking. If you would like to join me, visit my website www.TheTruePowerOfGirls.com to find out how you can donate this book to these girls.

If we could create a world where all girls know their true power, then we would have more fun in life. There would not be any bullies, and we would all be able to come together and embrace our differences. I would like to create this world together. We can all be inspirational leaders, have fun, and be brave, smart, powerful girls!

Grace DeLynne

Acknowledgments

First, I wish to thank my mom, Christine Gail. I probably wouldn't have done any of this without her help and encouragement.

I would like to thank all of my friends who supported me along the way. You know who you are.

I would like to acknowledge my dad, Dr. Chris Hengesteg, my sister Elizabeth, and my entire family for also being supportive. Thank you to everyone who helped edit and design my book.

I would also like to thank the people who have inspired me in my life: Emma Watson who was my first inspiration for writing this book, Renée Marino, Les Brown, Manny Lopez, leaders and teachers at my church, Jurgen and Leanne Matthesius, Christian Waples, the directors and team for the *Twisted* musical production, Dr. Lisa Dunne, and Pedro and Suzette Adao.

Last but not least, I thank God and my angel Grandma DeLynne who is always watching over me.

About the Author

Grace DeLynne is an inspirational speaker, actor, and dancer with a love for all things creative and fun. She began writing this book at the age of six and paused many times as she grew and learned first-hand about the true power of girls. Now as a tween, Grace loves inspiring young girls and women to discover their true power. Her heart's calling is to act in movies and to give her books away to underprivileged girls and girls coming out of human trafficking. She lives in San Diego with her parents, her sister Elizabeth, and her new Aussie puppy.

To learn more, to donate books,
or to connect with Grace for speaking or an audition, visit:

www.TheTruePowerOfGirls.com